Trees

by Maryellen Gregoire

Consultant:
Adria F. Klein, Ph.D.
California State University, San Bernardino

capstone classroom

Heinemann Raintree • Red Brick Learning
division of Capstone

Trees are the biggest plants in the world.

Trees are tall.

Trees have roots
to drink water.

Trees have trunks.
A trunk is a tree's stem.

Trees have branches with leaves.

Some leaves are flat.

Leaves change color in the fall.

The leaves fall
to the ground.

Most trees do not have leaves in winter.

New leaves grow in spring.

These trees have green leaves all year.

These trees are evergreens.

Evergreens have leaves that look like needles.

Evergreens have cones with seeds inside.

What kind of tree do you like?